How to Write a Script With Dialogue That Doesn't Suck

Vol.3 of the ScriptBully
Screenwriting Collection

by Michael Rogan

Published in USA by:

ScriptBully Press

© Copyright 2019 – Michael Rogan

ISBN-13: 978-1-970119-02-2

Table of Contents

Chapter 6: How to Make Sure Your Characters Don't All Sound the Same............61

Chapter 7: How to Cut and Mutilate Your Way to Kick-Ass Dialogue.......................69

Chapter 8: 3 Ways to Get as Good as the

Also By Michael Rogan

HOW TO WRITE A SCREENPLAY THAT
DOESN'T SUCK (AND WILL ACTUALLY SELL)

HOW TO WRITE A MOVIE SCRIPT WITH
CHARACTERS THAT DON'T SUCK

SCREENPLAY FORMAT MADE STUPIDLY
EASY

HOW TO SELL A SCREENPLAY IN THE 21ST
CENTURY

About the Author

Michael Rogan is a former Hollywood screenplay reader, optioned screenwriter and editor of ScriptBully magazine - an inbox periodical devoted to helping screenwriters write well...and get paid.

He is also the owner of the world's most neurotic Jack Russell Terrier.

And has made it his mission in life to rid the world of movies about trucks that turn into robots.

A Special FREE Gift for You!

If you'd like FREE instant access to my seminar "7 Secrets to a Kick-Ass and Marketable Screenplay" then head over to ScriptBully.com/Free. (What else you gonna do? Watch another "Twilight" movie?!)

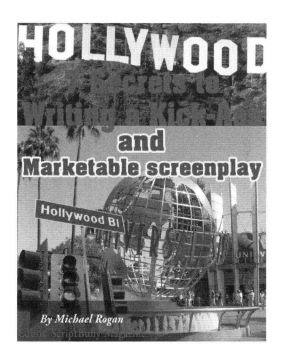

Prologue: "They're Gonna Talk to You and Talk to You"

"A great deal of talent is lost to the world for want of a little courage."

-Sir Phillip Sydney

I once did temp work for a Hollywood producer who'd say:

"Dialogue is like science fiction. When it's bad, it's the WORST thing ever. But when it's good, it's the best thing in the world.

"And careers ARE made."

And that's the truth.

Dialogue is the **ONE THING** people will

read in your script.

I know we all want to believe studio readers and production-company wage slaves pore over every piece of our scene description and scene headings and CROSS DISSOLVES and FLASHBACK sequences.

But it just AIN'T so.

Because dialogue is:

- The most readable and interesting thing in a screenplay.
- The part humans say (Which actors like)
- The quickest way to determine the "voice" of a writer

What This Book Promises

In a previous life, I used to teach acoustic guitar to eight-year-olds and suburban teenagers who thought they were Marilyn Manson.

I'll let you guess who was easier to work with.

And there always came a point when some

cynical high-schooler named Trevor — who wore skinny jeans and the same Iron Maiden t-shirt each time — would quit.

After one lesson.

Because he had just watched Dave Mustaine shredding on guitar in a YouTube video. And he realized he was never going to play guitar like that.

And I would tell him what I would tell every guitar disciple who wanted to quit, NOT EVERYBODY can "master" the guitar.

With its violin-like design, it's a very difficult instrument to play at a virtuoso level.

But it's easy to be "very good" at it.

You might never write dialogue like Aaron Sorkin, Diablo Cody, William Goldman, Larry Gelbart or Woody Allen or any other master of the form.

But you don't have to.

All you've gotta do is have your dialogue be "fun" for actors to say.

So, before you put any screenwriter on a

pedestal and mistakenly believe they have some key to a magical land where unicorns bestow them with mystical powers to write amazing dialogue, remember:

The same guy (Steven E. De Souza) who wrote "48 Hrs." and "Die Hard" - two of my personal all-time favorites - also wrote "The Flintstones."

And by following the steps in this book I promise, with 99.7% certainty, you will write better dialogue than "The Flintstones." (But then I'm sure you're already doing that now.)

Chapter 1:

What the #$% is Dialogue Supposed to Do Anyhow?

"Don't try to figure out what other people want to hear from you; figure out what you have to say."

-Barbara Kingsolver

If you've read a screenwriting book — throw a rock here in Southern California and you'll hit ten gurus working on one — then you've probably heard dialogue should do one of two things:

- Move the story forward
- Develop character

And if it doesn't do that, then you need to cut it. And that's all very nice. Except, I have no idea what that means.

"Move" the story forward?

"Develop" character?

This presumes people watch movies like they're running a marathon, fighting through the pain to reach some "goal" that involves electrolytes and searing knee tendinitis.

People watch movies for the thrilling experience of "watching the movie" not to check something off a to-do list. (That's what reality TV is for.)

Ever get out of the shower and put on the TV, and find your favorite movie is on and suddenly you're sucked into watching it for the next hour? (For me it's "The Shawshank Redemption." I can watch that anywhere, anytime.)

And you sit there on the edge of your bed, in your bath towel, waiting for your favorite scene.

You're waiting for that cool showdown, or that

devastating moment where everything is revealed. And guess what binds all of that together?

Kick-ass dialogue!

Because good dialogue (really) does three things:

- Offers actors the chance to say cool, unexpected zingers.
- Shows the different ways characters try to get what they want.
- Makes ordinary, real-life speech appear eloquent, funny and meaningful.

While it's nice we ask dialogue to do the heavy lifting of reinforcing our THEME and establishing our CHARACTER and furthering our PLOT...

Dialogue's main job should be creating cool, witty verbal battles that we wish we were smart enough to have in real life.

And that we're willing to sit in our bath towel for an hour just to relive, over and over again.

Chapter 1 Action Step: Take a Cue From the Masters

We will get to writing awesome dialogue. I promise.

First, though, let's look at how some of the masters have approached this craft.

I'd like you to pick out your three favorite movie scenes of all time. (I'm willing to bet my Taylor acoustic guitar that great dialogue is somewhere in those scenes.)

Now go watch those scenes again and look for:

The way dialogue is used as a back-and-forth BATTLE between characters to get what they want...and DEFEND what they already have.

The way the scene seems to **"turn"** on a line, or lines of dialogue (a zinger).

An exceptionally MEMORABLE line of dialogue that stands out. (And is super quotable.)

A certain line or series of lines that expresses a VIEWPOINT or perspective that resonates with you.

(Here's one of my all-time faves from "Broadcast News" by James L. Brooks.)

In the scene, Aaron (Albert Brooks) tries to convince his best friend, Jane (Holly Hunter), that she shouldn't be with the dashing, superficial head anchorman Tom (William Hurt).

```
                    JANE
     I have to be somewhere.

He looks at a clock reading 1:15 in
the morning.

                    JANE
     I told what's his name...Tom.
     That I'd meet him.

                    AARON
     Call him -- I mean it can wait,
     right?
```

                    JANE
               (now the plunge)
     I don't know. I may be in love
     with him.

                    AARON
               (as if he just burned
               his hand)
     No!!!!!

She starts for the door.

                    AARON
     Don't go.

                    JANE
     This is important to me.

                    AARON
     Yeah. Well...I think it is
     important for you too. Sit down.

She sits. He walks to a desk and

looks at her briefly.

Silence.

                    JANE
     What?

                    AARON
               (looking at her)
     Let me think a second. It's
     tough.

A remarkably long silence -- her mind
wanders, she takes stock...it is
evident that he is straining to get
it right, reaching into himself.

                    AARON
     Aaach...Jane...
               (glancing at note)
     Let's take the part that has
        nothing to do with me. Let's
        let me be your most trusted

friend, the one that gets to
say awful things to you. You
know?

                    JANE
          (testy and wary but fair)
Yes, I guess. Yes.

                    AARON
You can't end up with Tom
because it goes totally against
everything you're about.

                    JANE
Yeah -- being a basket case.

                    AARON
I know you care about him. I've
never seen you like this about
anyone, so please don't take it
wrong when I tell you that I
believe that Tom, while a very
nice guy, is the Devil.

JANE

(quickly)

This isn't friendship.

AARON

What do you think the Devil is
going to look like if he's around?
Nobody is going to be taken in if
he has a long, red, pointy tail.
No. I'm semi-serious here. He
will look attractive and he will
be nice and helpful and he will
get a job where he influences a
great God-fearing nation and he
will never do an evil thing...he
will just bit by little bit lower
standards where they are
important. Just coax along flash
over substance...Just a tiny bit.
And he will talk about all of us
really being salesmen.

(seeing he's not reaching
her)

And he'll get all the great
women.

She is getting pissed.

                    JANE
     I think you're the Devil.

                    AARON
     No. You know that I'm not.

                    JANE
     How?

                    AARON
     Because we have the kind of
     relationship…where if I were the
     Devil, you'd be the only one I
     told.

She's briefly impressed. He has a
point.

JANE

You were quick enough to get
Tom's help when...

AARON

Yes, yes. I know. Right. And
if it had gone well for me
tonight, maybe I'd be keeping
quiet about all this...I grant you
everything, but give me this...he
does personify everything you've
been fighting against...And I'm in
love with you.
        (realizing)
How do you like that? -- I buried
the lead.

I LOVE everything about that scene. But if I'm
forced to choose at gunpoint the things I love about
that scene:

- Their banter shows their different
  personalities: He speaks in qualifying

statements, she speaks in declarative statements.

- His dialogue shows him trying different strategies - logic, guilt, anger, revelation - to ultimately get what he wants.

- His argument for her being with him is not just about love, it's about the diminishing standards of broadcast media, and our consumerist culture. (Or is that just a ploy he's using to get what he wants?)

- The dialogue expresses a theme I can relate to: Why do all the great girls fall in love with the wrong guys? (Hint: What YOU respond to will be a theme you likely will want to write about.)

- Mostly, though, I love the line "How do you like that? -- I buried the lead." A great TV news industry metaphor that's clever, funny, and incredibly sad.

Now do the same for your three favorite scenes.

You might just be a little surprised by what you find. (And if your favorite scene is from a Michael Bay film, then God help you. There's nothing this book can do for you.)

Chapter 1 Key Takeaways:

- **Dialogue doesn't ALWAYS move the plot forward.** But it should always represent a character's viewpoint to get what they want.

- **Dialogue works best when it gives actors great lines and provides equally matched characters some ammunition.** Demonstrating theme and character growth will be a nice side effect.

- **When examining your favorite scenes of all time look for:** how dialogue is a battle, how dialogue is used by characters to get what they want and how scenes often "turn" on a single line of dialogue.

Chapter 2:

Writing Dialogue That Doesn' Suck

"Fiction reveals truths that reality obscures."
-Ralph Waldo Emerson

Okay, we've briefly touched on what dialogue SHOULD accomplish. Now let's go over what dialogue shouldn't do, ever. (Under any circumstances.)

And that is: Say exactly what's on a character's mind.

Two reasons for this:

- When characters say exactly what's on their minds, it's inherently undramatic. (And about as interesting as an insurance convention.)
- Human beings HATE being vulnerable. (And when characters reveal their innermost feelings, at the drop of a hat, it makes them less human.)

The irony is: The **more** characters try "not" to be vulnerable - the more they try to hide their true selves - the **more** interested we are in them.

You've probably come across the term "on-the-nose dialogue" in many overpriced screenwriting books.

This is the classic:

Bill: Are you alright, Jane?

Jane: No. I'm sad. I'm worried about our marriage. And what it might mean for the kids.

Would YOU want to act that scene? (Go on, I dare ya!)

There's no disconnect, no juxtaposition

between what a character thinks and feels and what's coming out of their mouths. And that's pure death for a scene.

Daytime soap operas often veer into this on-the-nose dialogue. But they have an excuse. (Sort of.)

They must simultaneously keep the action moving forward, at the same time they must give LOTS of exposition about what's been going on the last few weeks. (No telling when a viewer jumped on the weekday bandwagon.)

But do you really want to take a page from an episodic television form whose primary goal is to sell fabric softener?

Of course not.

You want to constantly focus on the disconnect between what a character feels…and what they say.

Because it's in the disconnect where the magic happens.

"Mind the Gap"

How do you bring some of that disconnecting magic to your dialogue?

Simple.

Find out the **one sentence that epitomizes what your character thinks, feels, wants, desires in a scene**. And make damn sure they NEVER say it.

Or if they say it, make damn sure it's the hardest thing they ever have to say. It took Jack Nicholson's character (Jake Gittes) in "Chinatown" slapping Faye Dunaway twelve times before she uttered the BIG secret in that film.

There are numerous examples of this done well, but here's one from "Sleepless in Seattle":

(In the scene, Tom Hanks' character Sam, explains to a radio talk show host how he and his son are doing after the death of his wife.)

                    SAM
Look, it's Christmas –
          (as the two of them sit down
       together on the bench)
Maggie – my wife. Always did it
big, she loved she really, I mean,
she loved, she made everything
beautiful. It's just tough this
time of year. (puts his arm around
Jonah) Any kid needs a mother.

He talks about Christmas, and his son, and the time of year. He talks about everything except the hard truth that is staring him in the face: "I miss my wife. And I don't know how I'm going raise this kid alone."

Doesn't matter if it's a romantic comedy or a Western; I defy anybody to watch the scene in "Lonesome Dove" where Gus and Woodrow say their goodbyes and do everything but say the three words they feel, "I love you," without shedding a tear.

Sounds like torture, doesn't it? Yeah.

Also makes for great drama.

Chapter 2 Action Step: Walk Over the Booby Traps

Okay, here's your assignment: I'd like you to write a scene.

In this scene, a couple is having dinner. They've only been going out for a couple of weeks, so things are all unicorns and rainbows.

Your job is to have one character tell the other "I love you." Only you can't use the words "I love you."

The scene doesn't have to be long — three pages max. Just write it with your character having to express those **three magical words** - without using those **three magical words**.

After you've done that, look over a scene you've written in the past. Not your favorite. Not where you feel you nailed it.

But one that's IMPORTANT to your story. (And one where you feel like the dialogue just lies there like a bulldog fart.)

See, if you can find the one piece of dialogue that epitomizes where the main character is coming from.

Now rewrite the scene in one of the following ways:

- **Have the other character express the sentiment that should have been uttered by their counterpart.** If you want your THEME revealed, make damn sure the villain or the sidekick express it. Not your main character.

- **Have a character say the ON-THE-NOSE line sarcastically**. Joss Whedon is a master at this.

- **Have a character use the sentence as a verbal attack against another character.** Remember: Nobody wants to be vulnerable. And that includes the crazy characters inside your brain.

Learning to write scenes where characters "dance" around the truth can be one of the most powerful things you can do as a writer. (And help you create scenes that audiences — and studio execs — remember for decades.)

Chapter 2 Key Takeaways:

- **Under NO circumstances should the characters in your scenes say what is EXACTLY on their mind.** Unless you're on the staff of The Young and the Restless.

- **Figuring out the ONE sentence that epitomizes a scene, and then writing everything but that sentence, is a great way to give your scene added emotional punch.** Not to mention it gives your writing a TON more focus.

- **If you MUST write the sentence that "explains all" be sure to use it sarcastically, as a weapon**, or said by the "wrong" character. Or as a recurring joke.

Chapter 3:

How to Steal Your Way to

Awesome Dialogue

"The secret to getting ahead is getting started."
-Mark Twain

There's a nugget of screenwriting wisdom that says no writer should try to write dialogue until they've firmly outlined their story and know their character's motivations inside and out.

Nonsense.

While it helps to know your characters to WRITE effective dialogue, sometimes it's in writing dialogue you learn WHO your characters are.

And the creative unconscious is not like a train schedule. If a cool line pops into your head, write the bastard down.

"I Have Always Depended on the Kindness of Strangers"

A couple of years ago, I was working on a romantic comedy spec script (yeah, I know, get in line), and I kept working on endless beat sheets and index-card outlines and 12-page character studies...you know...instead of writing crap down.

And then a simple exchange between my female lead and her friend popped in my head:

Friend: Just be yourself.

Female Lead: Can I be somebody else being themselves?

Bingo! I had the spine of my story nailed. Everything flowed out of that.

I KNEW she would spend most of the story trying to "be" somebody else, in this case literally impersonating a punk rock musician — don't ask, it's as contrived as it sounds — to win the love of her life.

Only to find out it isn't TRUE LOVE if you aren't being true to yourself. (Not profound, I know, but helpful.)

And it all came from a **single** line of dialogue.

Resist the temptation to WAIT to write dialogue. Even if you're not currently working on a script, I highly, highly, highly recommend you create a dialogue swipe file.

What the hell is a dialogue swipe file?

The term comes from advertising — yeah, those bastards — and relates to the practice of copywriters collecting swipe files of ads that they like and catch their attention. (Mostly so they can rip them off with their own ads.)

I'd like you to do the same. Your swipe file SHOULD comprise THREE lists:

List No.1: Cool Dialogue From Films, Plays, Books, Magazines and Newspapers

This is stuff you hear and just love from other sources. You CANNOT use this in your scripts.

But keep collecting this stuff and you'll get a sense of the rhythm of good dialogue. (And it'll trickle into your writing almost by accident.)

A few of my faves:

- "You're not too smart, are you? I like that in a man." — "Body Heat"

- "Rommel, you magnificent bastard. I read your book!" — "Patton"

- "Mrs. Robinson, if you don't mind me saying so, this conversation is getting a little strange." — "The Graduate"

But it doesn't have to just be from films, it could be from anywhere.

One of my favorite lines is from a local newscast of two 75-year old men who got into a fight at a dialysis clinic over a basketball game between Louisville and Kentucky.

Reporter: Why'd you punch that 75-year-old man in the face?

Kentucky Fan: He was meddlin' in my business.

Doesn't get much better than that.

List No.2: Random Crap You Hear People Say

From here on out, I am officially giving you permission to eavesdrop on people. Don't worry, it's not a felony. (Least not in most states.)

This will do two things:

- Show you that MOST people never say what's on their minds.
- Show you people are treasure troves of weird, cool dialogue.

This is real dialogue I've heard over the years and collected into my book:

- "I made a baby on this block." (While walking on Haight Street in San Francisco.)
- "Too much sports memorabilia in an adult male's house is not a good idea." (At a party.)
- "When it comes to love, I feel like I'm on the island of misfit toys." (In the break-room at my former job.)

They aren't amazing, and I don't know if I'll ever use them.

But what they have is REAL emotion behind them. And that's a great start when writing dialogue.

List No.3: Cool Stuff You Think Up

You can either combine this with list no.2 or make it a separate list. Whatever, it's your party.

But you want to get into the habit of jotting down lines you come up with.

Don't worry if you're not a master at this yet.

(You will get better at it with practice.)

If nothing comes into your head, just try to tap into things that make you FEEL something strong.

Just off the top of my head right now here are a couple of lines:

- "It's hard to love you if you never stop talking."
- "You sold my vintage "Star Wars" action figures at a garage sale. But I'm the jerk!"

Again...this isn't award-winning stuff. But we're not going for award-winning. We're just swimming with our dialogue floaties on right now and trying to find out what we like and don't like.

Chapter 3 Action Steps:

Decide on a collection device, whether it be a physical notebook, your iPad or your smartphone (I like to use the voice memo app on my iPhone) that will help you get into the habit of collecting:

- Quotes you overhear from strangers
- Quotes you love from movies and books you consume
- Quotes you come up with on your own

Shoot for trying to add at least one quote a day to each list. (Before you know it, your sub-conscious will seek this rich dialogue awesomeness all on its own.)

Chapter 3 Key Takeaways:

- **Do not WAIT to write dialogue until you have every piece of your story mapped ou**t. Forget what Robert McKee says…collect a dialogue swipe file. NOW!

- **One way to get good at dialogue is to collect your favorite lines from books, TV and film**. Don't plagiarize; you just want to get a feel for the rhythm of good dialogue.

- **Eavesdropping on other people not only isn't rude, but vital for writers**. Write down interesting, funny, strange, and insightful things you hear people say throughout the day.

- **Come up with a line or two of dialogue a day**. Don't worry if you suck at first, you'll get better at it. Promise.

Chapter 4:

If You Can Talk, You Can Write (Dialogue)

"If you've got something to say, say it. And think well of yourself while you learn to say it better."
-David Mamet

The number one dialogue complaint I hear from screenwriters:

"I've got a great story. Amazing characters. An ending that'll bring a generation to tears. But I don't know how to write dialogue."

You don't know HOW to write dialogue?

You mean, you've mastered the exceedingly

strange convention that is screenplay format (INT. BEDROOM – DAY, anybody?), but with writing down the words humans say, something you've been mimicking since you were six months old, you don't know how to do it?

Of course you do.

The problem is you've been "writing" dialogue instead of "saying" dialogue.

I call it the "Office Kitchen Syndrome."

"I See Dead People"

Ever worked in an office?

There always comes a time when tragedy befalls the office kitchen: Some miscreant forgets to clean their Tupperware, a vagabond steals somebody else's beef and broccoli, a repeat offender leaves his milk in the fridge past its "sell by date."

And it's someone's job, whether nominated or self-appointed, to post a public note to remedy the situation.

The note usually goes one of two ways:

Version 1:

Attn: ACME Employees

It has come to management's attention that certain full and part-time employees have been leaving their food stuffs in the refrigerator, an appliance provided by management on management's premises, beyond the point at which the food is edible.

This has led to complaints of noxious fumes emanating from the kitchen area — especially for those assigned to cubicles 1A-1C and has contributed to a lowering of the quality and standard of this professional, working environment that has been in operation since 2006.

Please remove your food from the refrigerator in a timely manner. (If this directive is not heeded, the consequence will be the necessary removal of the aforementioned refrigerator.)

Management

Or, there's **Version 2:**

Hey Guys,

The fridge is disgusting. (Six-month-old yogurt? Really?)

I know not everybody can smell it. But I can, because I

have to sit next to it. (Worse yet, clients can smell it when they walk through.)

Please be more courteous. This ain't a college dorm. (Last I checked.)

It's where you work. (You know, the place that helps you make your car payment.)

Thx!

-The Guy Who Has to Sit Next to Smelly Yogurt

Which one do you respond to more? (If it's the first one, then I know a fascinating career in accountancy that awaits you.)

And why's the second one better?

Because it sounds like a human wrote it, not some bounty-hunter robot stored in cryogenic freeze.

The best dialogue is that which doesn't "sound" like dialogue at all. It "sounds" like people having a conversation.

But screenwriters sometimes get themselves in trouble by thinking they have to put on their official "writing" hat when pounding out lines.

They think it has to SOUND literary. Does this sound literary?

(From "<u>Precious</u> aka Push")

```
            PRECIOUS
            (V.O.)
In a book I read, a lady escaped
to a halfway house. And the lady,
she asked the people there just
what a halfway house was. They
tole her, you is halfway between
the life you had and the life
you want to have...Thas nice. That
also mean I can't stay here
forever and that there is still a
ways to go. It be something to get
apartment of my own.
```

Wouldn't pass a single standardized English test. But it's some of the most powerful dialogue you'll ever come across.

If You Hate Writing Dialogue, Don't

Pro screenwriters spend years trying to make their dialogue sound like it wasn't written. If you're having trouble, don't write it.

Say it.

You can do this in many ways. Here are a couple of my favorite non-writing, dialogue-creating techniques:

Non-Sucky Dialogue Tip No.1: Use the Text-to-Speech Tool on Your Computer.

Most new computers have voice-recognition features built in. All you need is a headset microphone and turn your blathering into written text.

It won't format your text in proper screenwriting format, but you'd be amazed how quickly you can churn out pages by talking them.

If you're feeling particularly ninja, you could buy some good old Dragon Speak Naturally software. (Amazon Link:

http://scriptbully.com/dragonspeaks)

As someone who has battled tendinitis for years, I can attest this software works damn good. (And best of all, it will work with Final Draft screenwriting software.)

Non-Sucky Dialogue Tip No.2: Act Out Your Scenes on Your Smartphone or Digital Recorder

If, like me, you suffer from some serious ADD and don't like sitting in your chair for over four minutes, why not hit record on your iPhone/android device and just act out your scene?

This is the practice a lot of writing partnerships use. (And you'd be amazed how fun it can be.)

Any recorder will do. (I prefer mini-disc digital recorders, but I have a soft spot for extinct technologies.)

The key thing is to have SOMEBODY transcribe it for you. (I usually head over to a site like

Upwork to find a contractor who'll transcribe all my mp3s into manageable chunks.)

Best of all, crank up cool movie soundtrack music in the background — I'm partial to John Williams — and you'll "feel" like you're writing the most epic stuff in no time.

Non-Sucky Dialogue Tip No.3: Call Yourself (Maybe)

So, if you don't already have a Google Voice account, I highly recommend you sign up for the service.

It's FREE, and it can help you set up an LA area code that will help you be taken seriously as a working screenwriter.

One other cool benefit of Google Voice is the ability to "phone" in your scenes to your voice mail. Google Voice will send you an email with a transcription of what you said. Cool, right?

Chapter 4 Action Step: Find Your Inner (and Outer) Voice

Try writing a scene, either from your existing screenplay or a brand-new project, with one of these non-writing vocal technologies.

Try not to be too self-conscious when "talking" your scenes out. (Maybe save this one for the home office, not your local overpriced Starbucks.)

Who knows? You may like this method so much you never go back. (Some screenwriters, such as John Milch ("NYPD Blue," "Deadwood") haven't "typed" a script in years.)

Chapter 4 Key Takeaways:

- **If you hate writing dialogue, then don't.** Instead focus on "saying" your dialogue.

- **The best dialogue is that which feels natural and human.** And often breaks every rule of grammar.

- **One great way to get "natural" dialogue is to use vocal-recognition software, like Dragon Speak, to churn out your pages.** It might even help you write your scripts in a much faster time.

- **Another option is to use the recording function on your smartphone or tablet of choice.** You could even get somebody to transcribe it for you for super cheap at a site like Upwork.

- **For a super cheap, Lo-Fi option simply sign up for Google Voice and leave a message with your new dialogue.** The service will email you a transcript of your call — which you can then use in your script. (Leaving you more time for more important stuff — like re-watching the "Firefly" series.)

Chapter 5:

Writing Exposition That Doesn't Put the Reader in a Coma

"Hard writing makes easy reading. Easy writing makes hard reading."
    -William Zinsser

Exposition, in case you're not familiar with the term, is the (often) boring, but important, information you gotta have in your script.

It can also be some of the worst writing you'll ever do.

Horrible examples abound, but here's one:

```
        JIM
It's just not the same since
Caroline left me.


       MATT
Ah, yes. Caroline. Your wife of
eight years. Who you met at an
insurance seminar and is the
mother of your children and was
once engaged to the Prince of
Denmark. Yes, I remember.
```

Exposition is also called "laying track," as in "it's about as interesting as watching somebody lay railroad track."

My favorite story about exposition comes from Humphrey Bogart. The star of "Casablanca" is reputed to have said:

"If I ever have exposition to say, I pray to God in the back of the shot they've got two camels f%$#&ing."

Unless you plan on securing a couple of amorous camels, you must learn how to "disguise" your exposition in a clever, artful way.

How do you do that? There are three keys every film scribe should keep in mind with expository dialogue:

Exposition Key No.1: You Don't Need as Much Info as You Think You Do

I know you think you need to "establish" so many things with your character.

Their fear of intimacy, previous drug habit, unrequited love for the girl next door, a twelve-year stint as a circus clown.

But, and you'll have to trust me on this, a good actor/actress can convey most of that info with a look.

Did we really need dialogue to "establish" that there was something going on with Maria and Captain Von Trapp in "The Sound of Music"?

How about "Fatal Attraction?" Didn't we know something was "wrong" with Alex Forrest (Glenn Close) the moment we saw her?

If you focus your dialogue more on your characters trying to get what they want, and less on what happened to them in the past, the better off you'll be.

As viewers, we'll figure it out along the way, and there's nothing we like better, than having to figure it out along the way.

Exposition Key No.2: Use Exposition as a Weapon

Instead of having a character express "backstory" about themselves, have another character use that information against them. It's a much better, more interesting way to do it.

This scene is totally un-actable:

                    BILL
Julie, I love Candace. But what
with her history of mental
illness, and my predilection for
bad romantic choices, I'm still
not sure if it'll work out.

                    JULIE
I understand.

   Whereas:

                    BILL
Julie, I love Candace.

                    JULIE
Yeah. She's just your type: medicated
and emotionally unavailable.

   See how that information doesn't "feel" like
information. It "feels" like conflict. Which it is.
(And conflict is real good to have in a script.)

Tip No.3: Have the Villain Articulate the Theme of Your Script

If you've got to have a character provide the lowdown of what the story is about, and sometimes it's unavoidable, you better be damn sure it's not your hero spouting off.

This scene might get you admittance to the screenwriting hall-of-shame:

```
Batman and the Joker face off on top
of the Empire State Building.


                  JOKER
Why don't you just give up, Batman?
Batman motions to the panicked New
Yorkers who watch from the street
below.


                  BATMAN
  Because I believe people are good.
  Because I believe the human race
  is worth saving. And even if it
```

means I may die today, it will
have been a fight worth fighting.

Dear God, where's the barf bag? But switch it around and you'll have something infinitely more interesting:

                    THE JOKER
    Why don't you just give up,Batman?

Batman glances toward the panicked New Yorkers crowded below. The Joker notices.

                    THE JOKER
    Hold on. Are you telling me you
    actually "care" about these
    people? That you actually
    "believe" in the human race?
             (thinks)
    And they think I'm crazy.

See? By using the information as a weapon, you can sneak it in. And being sneaky is what being a screenwriter is all about.

Chapter 5 Action Step: Attack!

I'd like you to write a scene between an overbearing dad and his troubled son.

In the scene you should reveal:

- The son spent time in jail for going AWOL during boot camp.
- The son got a girl pregnant, and he hasn't spoken to either the girl or his child in years.
- The son is still in love with the girl.

Make sure all that info is conveyed:

- By the dad
- As a personal attack
- Visually, as much as possible

I know this will be hard. That's okay. Hard is good.

Then when you're done with that

father/son scene, see if you can give a facelift to an old scene of yours by having the antagonist deliver all the exposition as an attack.

Villains are always good for heavy lifting like theme revelation, motivation testing and anything involving camels.

Chapter 5 Key Takeaways:

- **Exposition is the background information readers and viewers need to understand your story**. It's also some of the worst writing on the face of the earth.

- **Exposition is best when used as a weapon**. Let a character's backstory be used against them by other characters.

- **If you can, do away with exposition entirely**. Trust your actors will be able to convey most information with a look.

- **Whenever possible, have the villain or antagonist express the BIG THEME of your stor**y. Don't, whatever you do, give it to your main character.

Chapter 6:

How to Make Sure Your Characters Don't All Sound the Same

"The truth will set you free. But first it will piss you off."

-Gloria Steinem

Of all the scripts I've read, and written coverage for, the biggest dialogue problem I come across is: All the characters in the screenplay sound like the same person. (And I'm willing to bet, that person is the AUTHOR.)

It's understandable, really. Who else are you supposed to sound like when you start out?

But if you want to make the jump from wannabe to professional, you've gotta learn to write outside your comfort zone.

And that means you must listen. (You know, to other people besides the voices in your head.)

"We've Got a Problem, Houston"

Confession: I grew up in a surfing town community in Southern California called Encinitas. To say it wasn't exactly a hotbed of ethnic and cultural diversity would be a fish taco-infused understatement.

And for a while, all my short stories and one-act plays sounded like a schizophrenic having an argument with himself. (Namely me.)

Then I had a writing teacher named Joe Sasway do me the biggest favor in the world.

He asked me to white-out the names on my script and see if I could tell who was speaking.

I applied the white-out, and I didn't have a clue who was talking. (They all sounded like pretentious versions of me.)

That's when Joe said it was time to hit the mall.

"Follow the Money"

The mall, Joe explained, was like a writer's research lab. You spend hours sitting at the food court, listening to the various, different ways that people communicate. (And mostly complain and talk crap about their friends.)

The 14-year-old skater punk talks one way. A family of Hasidic Jews talks another. A group of 12-year-old tween girls talk - well, not so much talk, as scream - a completely different way.

By listening to the various conversations going on around you, you'll pick up on different cadences and rhythms people have.

Linguists believe we use speech, not to communicate or be understood, but to elevate our status.

To make ourselves appear AWESOME and get what we WANT. (Sounds like every good film character I've ever seen.)

Try to get into the habit, no matter where you go, of starting to really LISTEN to the dialogue all around you.

Don't worry so much about dialects and accents. What you're focusing on is:

- How **extensive** is their vocabulary?
- Are they **wordy** or **succinct** in the way they speak?
- Is there **slang** or abbreviated words they use regularly? (Teenagers aren't the only ones who use slang.)
- Do they **emphasize** certain words over others?
- Do they **trail off** at the end of sentences? Or do they get **louder** the longer they talk?

Dialogue is rhythmic, no question about it. But

it's something you can develop an ear for.

And besides when else are you going to get permission to hang out at the food court on a Saturday afternoon?

Chapter 6 Action Steps: Go Shopping!

…for great dialogue, that is! (Sorry, couldn't help it.)

How does that woman with the facelift and Dolce and Gabbana bag sound different than the soccer mom who wears a hooded sweatshirt?

And how do people communicate? (Once you do this, you'll be shocked by how much people interrupt each other and don't listen to each other.)

Here's your assignment:

- Head to your local mall, with laptop or notebook in hand.
- Pick out three people at the mall, at random, and write a one-page monologue about them revealing their

deepest, darkest secret. (Make it hard for them to say.)

- Next, eavesdrop on a conversation and see if you can write what's NOT being said. Or, even better, write what comes next after their conversation. (You could even introduce another character into the scene that could disrupt the whole dynamic.)

Chapter 6 Key Takeaways:

- **Many newbie scribes write characters that all sound the same**. And THAT character is usually the screenwriter.

- **White-out the names on your scripts and try to pick out who is talking**. If you can't figure out who's speaking, then you may need to work on dialogue-listening skills.

- **Shopping malls are perfect for sharpening your dialogue skills.** Not to mention great places to get a churro.

- **When "listening" for dialogue at the mall focus** on vocabulary, intention, what's not being said and the words they emphasize.

- **Try to imagine each conversation you eavesdrop on is an actual scene**. What takes place after you? What happened before you came onto the scene?

Chapter 7:

How to Cut and Mutilate Your Way to Kick-Ass Dialogue

"Cut! Cut! Cut! Your reader has a life."
-M.E. Jerr

Want to know my favorite line of dialogue ever?

It's from "Escape From Alcatraz." A prison psychiatrist asks Clint Eastwood's character:

Prison Psychiatrist: How was your childhood?

Clint: Short.

Damn, that's good.

Much better than:

Prison Psychiatrist: How was your childhood?

Clint: It was difficult. My father didn't want me. And my mother...don't get me started on my mother. She was overbearing, but not in a loving sort of way, but in a...you know...overbearing sort of way that led to...

Throughout this book I have maintained you should let your dialogue freak flag fly.

That by placing artificial limitations on your dialogue creation you'll miss out on some serious gems.

This is because writing is like taking a road trip with Zooey Deschanel. It should be spontaneous, messy, and a totally right-brained activity.

But rewriting is like watching a sniper at work: cold, ruthless, and efficient. And when you've got dialogue that's emotional, powerful and lean, then you're ready to rule the world.

But to make it lean, you've got to trim the fat.

To help with your trimming, here are my five keys to rewriting dialogue and making yourself into a serious dialogue-writing machine:

Rewriting Tip No.1: Cut Out the Adjectives and the Adverbs

Adjectives and adverbs are not your friends. Trust me.

Saying: "I ruthlessly killed an obnoxious, overweight cop" is not as powerful as "I killed a cop."

Simple. To the point. Without fluff.

Tim Kazurinsky, a former regular on Saturday Night Live, remembers a guest host once yelling at the writers during a run-through:

"Don't give me so many f@$#ing adjectives! I'm the actor! I supply the adjectives!"

Let them supply them. It's their job.

And don't get me started on adverbs. They are the worst. (Stephen King is right when he says, "The road to hell is paved with adverbs.")

That's because adverbs are not ACTIVE. They "modify" action.

As screenwriters, we don't have time to "modify" anything. We gotta get RIGHT to the point! (And leave the modifying to all those novelists.)

Rewriting Tip No.2: Cut Out What Can Be Said With a Look (or an Action)

Now, you don't have to remove all your dialogue goodies. But it's your job to look for bits of dialogue that are more reaction than actual action.

Which do you think is more dramatic?

Boy: Are we breaking up?

Girl looks down. Trying to find the words. She looks out the window. Then back at him.

Girl: Yes.

CUT TO: Boy loading moving boxes into his 1986 Ford Fairmount.

or...

Boy: Are we breaking up?

Girl looks down. Trying to find the words. She looks out the window. Then back at him.

CUT TO: Boy loading moving boxes into his 1986 Ford Fairmount.

See, how much better that reads. And we may not even want to REVEAL the answer to the question that quickly.

This is USUALLY something I do in the rewriting phase. (I tend to write first-drafts where everybody says everything. Twice.)

But pull these weeds out in your rewrite and your script will sing.

Tip No.3: Remove the Most On-the-Nose Dialogue Line in Your Scene

We went over this in an earlier chapter, but if your main character desperately wants to say, "I love you," make damn sure they say everything in that scene but "I love you."

One simple way to do this is to literally write the "on-the-nose" line in the margin of the script.

(And then see how close I can get the characters to it, without saying it.)

Tip No.4: Contractions, Em Dashes and Dropped Pronouns are Your Friends

Maybe it's because people are lazy. But people rarely finish thoughts when they speak.

And if you write your dialogue with every word written out, and every speech complete, your work will sound like a Masterpiece Theatre episode. So...having your character say:

```
            JULIE
There was a man I once dated. He
was smooth and dashing. Sometimes
he would sing to me as we were
walking down the street. "Spanish
Harlem." And all the other girls
would look on with jealousy. I do
not think I have ever been
happier.
```

OR we could do:

```
          JULIE
There was this one guy. Smooth.
Sometimes he would…We'd be walking
down the street and he'd sing.
"Spanish Harlem," I think. Man,
you shoulda seen the other girls.
Daggers. Straight-up daggers in
their eyes. That was…those were
good times.
```

Tip No.5: Keep Your Speeches to Three Lines or Less

Now, I love a good monologue as much as the next guy. (Robert Shaw's description of the sinking of the USS Indianapolis in "Jaws" still gives me the chills.)

But long blocks of dialogue read like…long blocks of dialogue.

Make sure you break it up, either with description, a parenthetical, or another character's response.

Now when you're a professional screenwriter who's got a couple of sales under your belt, you can break this rule as much as you want.

But for now, split those monologues up.

They're boring to read.

And monologues don't happen. Unless my mother is doing one of her rants about the Democratic party.

Chapter 7 Action Steps: Size Matters

From now on, each time you go to rewrite scripts, pay attention to these areas of dialogue:

- Kill adjectives and adverbs.
- Remove anything that can be said with a "look."
- Remove the one, big on-the-nose line of dialogue.
- Embrace contractions and grammatical fragments.

- Break up your long speeches with other characters or scene description.

Chapter 7 Key Takeaways:

- **Writing dialogue should be spontaneous and free-flowing**. Rewriting dialogue should be ruthless, cold and calculated.

- **Avoid modifiers, such as adjectives and adverb**s, to make your prose leaner and tighter.

- **Cut any dialogue that can be expressed with a glance**. Don't worry there'll be plenty of places for your clever dialogue elsewhere.

- **Kill any dialogue that expresses the ONE THING that scene is about**. Repeat this throughout your script and you'll be amazed at how much better it'll become.

- **Leave your inner English teacher at home when rewriting dialogue**. Write for rhythm, not complete sentences.

- **Get rid of monologues**. They not only kill your pace, but script readers skip them anyway.

Chapter 8:

3 Ways to Get as Good as the Pros

"If anything terrifies me, I must try to conquer it."
-Francis Chichester

If you've followed the steps in this book, there's only one thing to do with your dialogue. And that's to write a bunch of it...and then get your stuff read.

Out loud.

Even the best, most finely crafted and honed speech will expose its flaws and vulnerabilities when read out loud.

And that's the point. You want to hear what it sounds like. (When real humans say it, not just when you skim through it on your Dell laptop.)

Now, this next step can be scary. I get it.

It was scary for me too.

I remember hearing my words for the first time being read in an Intro to Playwriting class and getting that sinking feeling in my stomach because I'd just realized (too late) that I had my characters say the SAME THING, over and over and over...

But once you've had a chance to do some rewriting, you've picked away your adverbs and your on-the-nose dialogue, it's time to dig in and give your dialogue a test-drive.

Here is my three-phase process for ensuring your script's dialogue is as sharp and awesome as can be before sending it out into the great unknown:

Phase 1: Record Yourself Reading Aloud

I know. You hate the sound of your own voice.

Welcome to the club.

Everybody hates the sound of their own voice. Everybody thinks they sound nasal-y and awful and whiny. Except for actors and actresses. (They think they sound supremely awesome.)

But this one exercise alone will be SO helpful it'll astound you.

Here's what you do:

- **Choose a recording device.** (I like to do this at my desktop — more comfortable — so I like to use FREE programs like Audacity and Garage Band to record my audio.) But you can use anything you want.

- **Break it up into chunks.** Especially if you're reading a full-length script. You will absolutely go bonkers if you don't.

- **Read through your script.** Or scenes, depending on the length of work you've done.

- **Burn your audio to a CD or throw an mp3 on your audio-listening device of choice**. I prefer to listen while driving, but totally up to you.

- **LISTEN to the dialogue**. Don't focus on the "performance." You're not doing an audition, you're just trying to get a sense of the realism and rhythm of the dialogue.

I know this doesn't sound like a big deal. It is.

Other screenwriters don't do this. (At least not the ones you're competing against.)

Doing this just a few times will QUICKLY help you hone in on the parts of your dialogue that sing majestically and which lie there like a poodle fart.

Anything you trip over verbally is an area that needs rewriting. Anything that sounds natural and right is a keeper. (This exercise is also fan-tastic for sharpening your screenplay description skills.)

Once you've finished Phase 1, it's time to move

on to:

Phase 2: Schedule a Staged Reading

Oh, God. You mean, I'm going to ask other human people to listen to your words?

Yeah. Scary. I know. But it's the absolute BEST thing you can do for your writing. Hands down!

As a former playwright, I loved staged readings. First, hearing people actually "say" the words you write can be as addicting as government-grade opium.

Secondly, there's no better B.S. Detector for figuring out what works and what doesn't in your script than a staged reading.

Staged readings can show you:

- If a joke is funny or not. (Most of the time, not.)
- If you've put too much dialogue in a scene. (The answer is YES!)

- How three pages in a script is an eternity.
- If your character dialogue all sounds the same. (It will, at first.)
- If your syntax (the order of words) is awkward. (Most time it be, yes!)

How do you do this without paying anybody?

Simple. Go down to your local community college or polytechnic drama department and tell them you'd like to do a staged reading. (You'll provide the food and drink.)

Tell them you've got a feature-length screenplay you'd like to workshop. (Actors love the expression "workshop.")

If you've ONLY got a scene or two, have a couple other screenwriter friends bring their scenes over too, and you could do a group reading.

Record the staged reading and listen to it repeatedly. This is more valuable than a graduate degree in screenwriting. (I've got the student loans to prove it.)

Phase 3: You Vs. The Pros

I must warn you: this phase is staggeringly effective. (And it might be the most powerful exercise in this here entire book.)

It's also the most dangerous. Because, if not approached carefully, it can send you into a writer self-esteem tailspin, and have you giving up your writing dream faster than a Lindsay Lohan relationship.

Now, I wish I could take credit for this tip. (I really do.) But it came from a buddy of mine who learned it in UCLA film school.

But what you do is:

- Pick out a dialogue-heavy scene from your script.
- Find a scene from a produced film of the same genre — that was made in the last five years — and roughly the same length as your scene.
- Listen to the produced scene and note

> how many jokes, zingers, turning points,
> verbal attacks, etc.

- Listen to your scene and note the same thing.
- Figure out how your scene stacks up.

Like I said, this can be dangerous. In the wrong frame of mind you end up beating yourself up that your scene has 34% less jokes than that scene from "Silver Linings Playbook."

But you gotta remember: Many people work on developing a screenplay before it reaches the theatres (Even the scene you're watching didn't start out that way). And the exercise is only to give you a benchmark — something to shoot for.

Now you don't have to do this for every SINGLE scene in your script, but for those big emotional scenes or comic set pieces, it's helpful to KNOW what screenwriting success looks like.

Whenever I do this exercise, I usually find:

My dialogue is too logical, meaning one thought leads to another, which is the kiss of screenwriting death.

My dialogue answers too many questions. Most good dialogue is about misdirection and covert "strategery."

I don't have enough meat on the page. Most scripts have three jokes, zingers, or mini-turning points per page, (I do not understand why this is; just seems to work out that way.)

But don't take it as an indictment of your talents. Remember: the ending to "Casablanca" got rewritten five times. (Including the night before the scene was shot.)

And if those masters of the dialogue form didn't know what they were doing at first, then it's okay for you to encounter initial trouble.

Chapter 8 Key Takeaways:

- **It's hard to know if your dialogue is any good until you HEAR it out loud.** Scary as that thought may be.

- **Recording yourself speaking your dialogue** — and scene description — can be a fantastic way to find out what's working. (And not working.) Don't freak over your voice. You're not an actor, you're a writer!

- **Setting up a staged reading of your work, with local actors, is my favorite way to put your writing to the test**. Pay close attention to audience reactions and which words the actors stumble over.

- **One of the best, if frightening, ways to sharpen your dialogue is to see how it compares to a similar scene in a produced fil**m. Don't be overly critical. Just approach it like a scientist. What does your scene need to do to stack up?

Epilogue:

This Hero Stuff Has Its Limits

"You only live once. But if you do it right once is enough."

-Mae West

"The ability to write dialogue can't be taught."

How many times have you heard that?

Or how about…"some people either have an ear for writing dialogue or they don't."

That's another good one. Thing is: They're true.

We're not sure if it's a genetic thing, or something the mothers of professional screenwriters ate during pregnancy. But what's clear is some writers simply "have" the ability to write great, witty, fascinating, interesting dialogue...

And some writers don't.

Except here's the thing about screenwriters who write kick-ass dialogue.

They used to suck.

Badly.

Case in point: Joss Whedon.

I loved "Buffy, the Vampire Slayer." Thought "Firefly" was the most interesting, unique sci-fi show ever on television. And I still believe "Dr. Horrible's Singalong Blog" is the most magical thing a human brain has ever conceived.

The man is a brilliant writer, and a master of witty, clever dialogue. He can do no wrong.

Except, I've read his first spec screenplay, "Suspension."

This script, described as "Die Hard on a Bridge," is...how do I say this...not as eminently fascinating as his other projects. (And I think I'm being kind.)

This rather pedestrian script, with overwritten dialogue and pretentious speeches, was the first spec he SOLD. For $250,000. (Just imagine for a second the material he wrote but showed nobody.)

If you're writing dialogue and feel you're not "getting it," don't worry. By doing it, you're "getting it."

You may never write dialogue as well as Eric Roth or Joss Whedon. But by following the steps in this book you'll get better, FAST.

Then one day you'll write dialogue that, ever so slightly, sounds like it's coming out of somebody's mouth. (And not your MacBook Pro.)

So keep at it. Get better. Rinse and repeat.

And, who knows, maybe we'll be quoting your dialogue fifty years from now.

Unlike other areas of screenwriting — yes, I'm talking to you screenplay format — dialogue is the absolute most fun thing about screenwriting. (Even on its worst day, it's still pretty darn good.)

And when it's cooking, when two characters are in a witty, verbal battle that seems to just leap off the page, well...there are few things in life better. (Except maybe watching a Michael Bay movie "bomb." That's pretty good too.)

Good luck with your writing. And if you've enjoyed this book, drop me a line at Michael@scriptbully.com.

Printed in Great Britain
by Amazon